The Gift of Julian of Norwich

TEXT BY KAREN MANTON
ILLUSTRATED BY LYNNE MUIR

AmP ave maria press
Notre Dame, IN
www.avemariapress.com

Published in the U.S.A. by Ave Maria Press, Notre Dame, Indiana, 46556

International Standard Book Number: ISBN: 1-59471-050-3

www.avemariapress.com

Text introductions and compilation: © Copyright 2005 Karen Manton
Illustrations and design: © Copyright 2005 Lynne Muir

First published in Australia by John Garratt Publishing

Typesetting: JamesGrechDesign
Printed by Tien Wah Press, Singapore

Translations are by Karen Manton from the texts published in *A Book of Showings to the Anchoress Julian of Norwich*, Vol.2. Edmund Colledge and James Walsh eds. Pontifical Institute of Medieval Studies, Toronto, 1978. Quotations in Middle English are from the same edition, reproduced with permission.

With thanks to Garry Eastman, Lynne Muir, Dr Ann Sadedin, Jill Manton, and Dr Graeme Garrett

CONTENTS
INTRODUCTION 5

Alle shalle
be wele,
and alle
shalle be wele,
and alle maner
of thynge
shalle be wele.

J ulian of Norwich lived during the late fourteenth and early fifteenth century in Norwich, a busy port and lively centre of trade on the east coast of England. For many years she was a recluse—an anchoress—living a contemplative life in the 'anchorhold' dwelling attached to the church of St Julian in the Parish of Conisford, Norwich. To our knowledge, she was the first woman to write a book in the English language: *Revelations of Divine Love*, also known as *A Book of Showings,* which exists in a short and long version (the Short Text and the Long Text).

The text records a series of sixteen visions or 'showings' that Julian experienced in 1373 during a severe illness. She was thirty years old. The visions are grounded in Christ's Passion and give intensely emotional, graphic descriptions of his pain and death. These showings inspired further bodily, intellectual and spiritual visions.

In response to this experience, Julian's desire was to record the showings so truthfully, that readers would feel as if they themselves have received the visions and the accompanying sense of being enfolded in love. Against remarkable historical and political odds, her text has survived to fulfil her wish.

In recent years her revelations have sparked renewed interest in theological and literary circles for her poetic use of language, strong feminine voice and keen theological insight.

She is becoming increasingly popular for modern readers. Amongst other reasons, this is perhaps because of her

understanding of God as an inclusive being, as both mother and father, the ground of all things, the all-encompassing environment of love in which everything exists.

Julian is also appreciated for her realism. She understands that 'for the time of our life, we have in us an amazing mixture of well and woe'. She receives the assurance that 'all shall be well', and she will not 'perish', but this does not eradicate her experiences of trouble, distress and pain.

Julian's insights are not confined within particular political, sexual, religious or cultural borders. While she worked within a Christian framework, Julian's understanding of God is universal, profound and simple. It has survived varying tides of thought, historical conflicts and political change. Her wisdom crosses many human-made boundaries of her day and ours.

The contemporary world is remarkably different from Julian's day. However, at the fundamentally human level people continue to seek love, goodness, peace and a sense of inner fulfilment, in the face of experiences that cause distress. We still ask the same questions as Julian: how shall all be well, how will there be peace when there is so much suffering?

Over the centuries, the *Showings* have brought comfort and understanding to people from all walks of life, who, like Julian, live in a mix of well and woe. *The Gift of Julian of Norwich* seeks to offer an inspiring glimpse into this fourteenth century woman's wisdom.

6

PART ONE

Julian of
Norwich
her Voice and
her World

In many ways Julian is an enigmatic figure because the details of her education, her family, her daily life, her entry into the anchorhold and her death are not recorded or discovered. We do know that she lived in troubled times of wars, crusades, uprisings and devastating epidemics.

Political and religious unrest was creating a turbulent world. The Hundred Years' War with France began in 1337, and the Great Schism began in 1378, with a new Papal seat at Avignon opposing Pope Urban VI of Rome.

Norwich was also a focus of tumult. Henry Despenser, the Bishop of Norwich, crusaded against the enemies of Pope Urban VI and brutally quashed an uprising in Norwich which was part of the Peasants' Revolt of 1381. He campaigned against Wycliff and his followers (known as 'Lollards') from 1397 onwards. Thomas Arundel (Archbishop of Canterbury and Chancellor of England) did not suffer religious or political difference, campaigned against Wycliffites and introduced a constitution in 1408 that included a ban on women teaching and on the translation of the Bible into the vernacular.

The plague was also devastating England. Norwich was besieged with three episodes during Julian's life-time, in 1348-49, 1361, and 1369. The population was halved. Failed crops and cattle disease created added hardship.

Julian does not mention any of these events or threats. However, her emphasis on love and unity is perhaps more urgent because of the politics around her. Her repeated statements that the revelations are in line with Holy Church, and her self-description as a humble creature 'unlettered'—both expected conventions from a medieval Christian writer—also reflect an awareness of the dangers, particularly for a woman, in speaking about religion with too much authority or innovation.

Assuming that the recorded date of Julian's illness at age thirty in 1373 is correct, Julian was born near the end of 1342 or the beginning of 1343. Her christened name is unknown. Anchorites usually took the name of the patron saint of their church. While some writers claim Julian might have been a nun, others disagree and suggest she might have been a widow who lost both husband and child in the plague. These details remain a mystery, however it is likely that she had close links with the Benedictine house at Carrow outside Norwich because this community held the benefice of St Julian's Church, Conisford and would have influenced decisions about who occupied the anchorhold.

Exactly when Julian entered the anchorhold is uncertain. Some people believe that she was living with her family when she received the visions, because she mentions that her family were waiting anxiously by her sickbed. Others argue that friends, family and clergy would have visited Julian in the anchorhold if she were seriously ill.

A number of texts and wills refer to 'the anchoress Julian' who is thought to be the author of the *Revelations of Divine Love*. In the Short Text's preface the scribe writes that Julian was living as an anchorite in 1413. Thomas Edmund left money to the recluse and her servant Sara in a will dated 1404. Some time between 1413 and 1415, Margery Kempe, a woman from Lynn who had a scribe record the story of her own life (*The Book of Margery Kempe*) visited Norwich to speak with 'Dame Julian' at the anchorage. She was seeking comfort and advice, and commented that Julian was well known for her wise discernment. John Plumpton's will of 1415 left money to the anchorite Julian, her maid, and a former servant Alice. The 1416 will of Isabel Ufford is perhaps the last reference to the author Julian of Norwich.

While Julian's contemporary Margery Kempe left a book that is full of her own personal details, Julian instructs her readers to turn their gaze from herself to God and gives very little detail about her personal daily life or business. Margery seems anxious to validate herself through her visions and life experiences and has left us a lively account of a woman's life in her time. Julian was more concerned with leaving a spiritual guide that speaks to all people and leaves us wondering about her personal life.

Life in an Anchorhold

Anchorites and the practice of living in an anchorhold grew out of the eremetic tradition. 'Anchorite' comes from a word meaning 'to withdraw' and was at one stage interchangeable with hermit. Gradually the word was used to refer to 'enclosed' recluses. In the *Ancrene Wisse*, a book written for anchorites, the anchorhold and its recluse are said to be 'anchored in God' and are likened to an anchor for the church so that waves or storms do not overturn it.

The anchorhold was usually attached to a church, which benefited both the anchorite and the people of a town. The recluse was offered safety, plus provisions of food and clothing from the church, while the local community and visitors had a resident spiritual advisor. The size of anchorholds ranged from one room or cell, to a house with a garden.

The role of an anchorite carried social and spiritual respect. People had to apply to the Bishop to become an anchorite. When a person entered this space, there was a special ceremony, including either a Mass of the Holy Spirit, or a Mass of the Dead. The anchorite might even be carried from the church to the anchorhold, as if dead. The priest sprinkled earth on the anchorhold floor, as a symbol that the person had 'died' to this life, and would 'rise' to another—the life of an 'enclosed' contemplative. In some cases the front door was even sealed over, like a tomb. Anchorites usually fulfilled their position until they died.

Some scholars regard the anchorhold as a kind of 'prison' or a form of social 'enclosure,' particularly for women. This may have been so in some cases, and the symbolism of the anchorhold and the entry ceremony are strongly reminiscent of Christ's tomb.

However, Julian's learned, creative and in many ways free-thinking text is also evidence that an anchorhold could be a 'womb' space of privacy, spiritual growth, intellectual activity and creativity. The anchorite could develop and be nurtured in ways that were often impossible otherwise. Far from restricting a woman, it may have offered freedom from other social options such as marrying, bearing children or living in a convent.

The life of an anchoress allowed a woman to read books, meditate and to think freely—at least within her own space. It seems a preferable option to the frustration of Margery Kempe who continually struggled to be a celibate pilgrim despite bearing many children and supporting a husband she did not like.

While living a reclusive life-style, anchorites played a significant role in the life of their church and associated religious communities. The anchorhold had a 'window to the world' where people could come for advice or encouragement, as did Margery Kempe. Some anchorites also taught children elementary secular and religious education at their window—young girls who could not go to school might take this option. It is also thought that some anchorites taught through convent or monastery schools (leaving the anchorhold for this duty). The anchorhold usually had a window into the church and might also have a window inside, between the dwelling of the recluse and the servants' work area.

Anchorites were not always alone in the anchorhold. Some anchorholds housed more than one recluse, and an anchorite could have a maid and a servant. Priests might also come to discuss spiritual matters or instruct the anchorite.

There are various books of instruction for anchorites and one of

the most famous of these, the *Ancrene Wisse* (mentioned above) was written by a monk for female anchorites. The guidelines cover spiritual matters and daily living. The author tells anchorites not to make their window a centre for gossip, and to hang a curtain over it so they do not gaze at men in the street and are not gazed at themselves. They should wear simple, comfortable, warm clothes, eat healthy vegetarian food, avoid fasting, and keep only one cat to catch mice and rats. A cow is not advised, as it might escape and wander around town being a nuisance.

A Book of Showings

There are several manuscripts of the *Showings* in England and one in Paris. The surviving Long Text manuscripts were copied in the sixteenth and seventeenth centuries. There is also a Short Text and excerpts of the *Showings* are found in manuscripts containing other mystical works, dating from the fifteenth century onwards.

Scholars have different opinions about the order in which the Short Text and Long Text were produced. It is thought that Julian composed the Long Text between 1388 and 1393, because she says that after the visions she spent fifteen to twenty years contemplating their meaning and interpretations.

Many scholars believe the Short Text was recorded immediately after the 1373 visions, as the content seems more immediate and less developed in some ways than in the Long Text and Julian seems less confident in her own authority as a writer. An alternative view is that the Short Text which refers to 1413 is the second version, heavily edited in response to Archbishop Arundel's restrictive laws, so that Julian, then seventy years old, was less at risk of persecution.

Whichever theory about the texts is correct, there seems to be both anxiety and the determination of a woman writer and teacher in Julian's position: 'because I am a woman should I not tell you the goodness of God?'

Julian is adamant her work supports Church teachings, although her ideas and language might have been politically sensitive to some ears. She was a woman not just speaking of God, but developing a sophisticated theological framework, and expressing it in the English language, incorporating translations of the Vulgate Bible and other significant religious texts. While acknowledging sin and damnation and professing to adhere to Church teaching on these matters, she nevertheless claims that sin has no substance in itself, and notes that she did not see Hell or any damned souls in her visions, though she believes in both.

In a literary and philosophical sense Julian's *Showings* must have been a challenge. Julian has woven her own content, style and interpretations together with ideas, writing methods and styles from texts in other languages, into one document in the English language. She did this with remarkable skill, at a time when English literature was newly emerging. She has earned praise from theologians and literary scholars alike, as a significant author and thinker.

Having survived any Catholic suspicions of being too liberal or too similar to Lollard thought during her own time, surviving manuscripts of the *Showings* were later under threat from new tides of Protestantism that found Julian's work too Catholic! Various Brigattine and Benedictine monasteries copied and saved the manuscripts from destruction by having them smuggled to Europe. Now all the manuscripts except one have returned to England.

Despite various religious restrictions and political upheavals, a wonderful range of creative artwork, architecture and literature emerged during Julian's era. Elaborate manuscripts, stained glass windows, masonry, metalwork and many other arts were flourishing with the establishment of monasteries and the support of libraries. The campaign to mirror the Holy City of Jerusalem in cathedrals and churches produced magnificent artworks and architecture. There was also an inspiring 'trade of ideas' between cities and ports such as Norwich.

Julian's work reflects this creativity and exchange of ideas. Her text is a complex, inter-woven artwork of various meanings, visual experiences, words, and references to other texts. Her use of rhetoric and her familiarity with texts in Latin and the vernacular, including the Bible, medieval and classical texts, indicate a well-educated and highly intelligent woman. Her text demonstrates that Julian was extremely well versed in Scripture, drawing mainly on the Gospels, the Johannine Epistles, Hebrews and the Psalms. As already noted, she appears to have translated from the Latin Vulgate Bible, but she might have had access to English Biblical translations as well.

With the proximity of libraries, numerous religious houses and the frequent visits of prominent religious thinkers and writers to Norwich, Julian would have been exposed to various streams of thought and ideas, as well as different texts. Julian gives one quote, from St Gregory, but scholars see a myriad of influences in her work, including Augustine, Dionysius, Bernard of Clairvaux, Thomas Aquinas and William of St Thierry. It is highly likely that she had access to Chaucer's *Boethius* and Langland's *Piers Plowman*, and similarities have been drawn between Julian's ideas and those in Marguerite Porete's *Mirror of Simple Souls* and Birgitta of Sweden's *Revelations*. Elements of Benedictine, Franciscan, Dominican and Carmelite

traditions as well as the renowned mysticism of the German Rhineland and Low Countries have also been noted in her work.

STYLE AND PURPOSE OF WRITING

Julian's revelations are thus a rich tapestry of words and ideas, repeated and woven in layers of meaning and symbolism. Julian uses repetition and words that connect to other texts as constant reminders of the key concepts she is teaching. It is a clever method of using words that set off a chain of thought and associations, helping people to absorb what is said and make relevant connections. These days we can search the internet using words and phrases to find a list of related links. Julian's text provides a similar function, with key words, ideas and phrases leading to a wealth of avenues for further meditation, discovery and connection, making it a remarkably 'interactive' text for the reader.

This style of writing and developing ideas creates inter-related threads and labyrinths. All things are mutually enfolded and moving in a circle with directions heading both ways. This is fundamental to Julian's way of seeing the world. She does not have one way channels. She uses multi-layers, multi-frequencies, multi-systems of meaning, symbolism, language and experience. This array of meanings and paths has made her text transportable through the centuries and between various traditions. Different people are stirred and inspired by different layers, and make their own connections.

As much as Julian's writing is wonderfully complex, it is also simple and 'homely' in feeling and words. Fascinating to people whose interest is theology, literature and mystical tradition, the *Showings* also speak to the hearts and minds of people who are attracted to a simple interpretation of love and goodness.

Julian's friendly way of speaking reflects not so much a lack of education (as some have suggested), but rather an ability to write for 'everyone in general', not just theologians. She is a master of language, intellect, and creativity, determined to make the love of God understandable to all.

When she received her visions, Julian noted how deeply stirred she felt for her 'even cristen'—her fellow women and men. This feeling of connection with others and concern for people's well being was the inspiration for her to write and spend years pondering how she would explain the revelations. At one point when she thought she would die, Julian's sorrow was not so much death as the missed opportunity to share her visions.

This desire to write was part of her deep sense of connection with humanity. Julian assures her readers that she is not more important than others because she received the visions, nor are the revelations for her alone. She believes that through her 'oneing' or unifying with God, she is equal and united with all humankind. We are all one soul, one human. The *Showings* are for everyone.

THE MYSTIC JOURNEY

It might seem unusual to modern readers that Julian asked God for her illness, but in medieval times, sickness was often seen as a journey into a new spiritual awareness, or as a way of being closer to Christ's suffering on the cross.

Women's bodies were often portrayed as 'negative', attached to sin, temptation, death and the earth, while men were believed to be more attached to reason. However, the growing interest in imitating Christ's body opened the way for women's bodies to take on a different role. Some theologians claimed women could draw closer to

Jesus than men, because the bleeding, suckling and birth-giving bodies of women mirror the body of Christ crucified.

Spiritual writings and experiences of medieval women— especially continental European mysticism—were often body-centred and associated with physical suffering. It is possible that through their physical and intellectual mystic experiences women gained a new authority to speak and write books for circulation. Certainly numerous women mystics and writers began to emerge at this time, speaking with their own voice while also remaining to varying degrees within the accepted and expected hierarchies and traditions of the Church.

Julian's work differs from many of the continental styles of erotic and ecstatic mystical writings. She has an intellectual approach which balances her understanding of physicality and humanity, claiming that both the soul and body of a human are grounded in the divine and together mirror the Trinity, and claiming that both reason and love must be engaged in understanding and experiencing God.

Thus Julian creates a balance between what is known as the 'negative way' and the 'positive way' of mysticism. The first way claims that God is mystery unfathomable, unknowable by the intellect. God cannot be known by thought, only love. It is an 'unknowing' way of knowing God, not helped by images, symbols or reason. This tradition is seen in the anonymous work *The Cloud of Unknowing* and various other mystical writings, and stems from Dionysius who believed that God is like a cloud, or an unknowable darkness.

The 'positive way' has a more tangible approach, using concrete images and symbols. God and the self can be known to some extent through reason, although the mystery of both remain. The focus of understanding existence is Christ's Birth, Passion and Resurrection— all deeply human experiences. Joy, love, fear and sadness are integral to the divine-human encounter. This was the kind of spirituality taught by Bernard of Clairvaux.

Julian's text is very close to the ideas of St Bernard, however she

also explores the unknown depths of God. In her revelations, which she sees as 'bodily sights', 'words formed' in her understanding, and 'ghostly' (spiritual) sights, Julian is shown many aspects of God and her own existence, but numerous unseen mysteries are still not revealed, while other showings are too complex for her to explain fully.

Aspects of the *Showings* reflect medieval literature in words and style. Julian's descriptions of Christ as a spouse and courteous lover echo poetry about the lover knight in courtly love poems and the Christ knight of religious poems. There are also parallels with dream and visionary literature, where the protagonist faces challenges on a journey that result in significant change and transformation. Julian's visions take her to the edge of death and suffering, where she is led into the ultimate point of love and goodness, and she herself is changed for ever.

Julian's Way

Julian's theology is centred on love, unity and balance, which seems quite the opposite of what was happening in some areas of politics and religion around her. She teaches love and acceptance in a time of war, censorship and division. Her writing is grounded in love, the Passion and the Trinity, and the belief that all things are united, interconnected and enfolded in God. She balances the positive and the negative, but not as binary opposites.

Julian intertwines all things, bringing various elements, attributes, visions and interpretations into a balance of three. Her visions come to her in three ways, with three main kinds of understanding. Words, images and interpretations are connected in threes, which she often relates to the three persons and one truth of the Trinity.

This pattern and framework is repeated throughout the *Showings*. It is as if Julian uses three spools around which to entwine, interconnect and weave the threads of her words, ideas and knowing. The intricate layers, patterns, echoes and images of her work are all imbued with this lattice of three. She desires three 'graces' as a gift from God, her visions come to her in three ways, she sees three degrees of bliss for every soul in heaven, words come to her in groups of threes and so on.

One of the most important examples of this is Julian's concept of 'being, increasing and fulfilling.' By 'being' Julian means the human's created essence of being which is made by and of God. This is 'increased' through being 'knit' to Christ, and 'fulfilled' in the work of the Holy Spirit. All three workings operate together in the ultimate restoration of humanity to 'bliss' in God.

This process is experienced through what Julian calls 'beholding'—a looking, longing and holding of something to the point where meaning is absorbed—and through 'oneing' (or unifying) and 'knitting' to God. In the practice of beholding and the act of being 'oned' or 'knitted' to God, a person comes to understand how all things are interconnected, and of the substance of God who will make all things well.

In this deep experience and understanding, Julian's visions, messages and showings are drawn together. Beholding and 'oneing' are like breathing in the experience, the understanding, the love, and an awareness of oneness with God, who is good. In this way, the essence of God is imparted and taken in, like osmosis. By sitting immersed in this love, we become love ourselves. We are inter-woven into God.

For Julian, this oneness is the original and most natural state of being. Julian calls readers to experience this interconnection, to be aware, to understand that God is. Regardless of the state we are in, our being is dwelling in God, in well and in woe, even in sin.

For Julian, sin is not a deed, or a severance from God that is blameworthy. Rather, sin is unnatural, in that it is not how we are meant to be. It is a ditch, a valley, a state that humans enter or fall into where they cannot see God. It is a cause of pain and woe, but in the end sin will be brought to nothing. As it is that which is not of God, sin has no substance (God being the ultimate substance). And as humans are made of God's substance, sin is not an original state for humans. It is a confusion, a distortion, a place or state humans enter as a result of their changeability.

This is illustrated in Julian's famous parable of a servant who rushes off to do a task for his lord. On the way the servant falls into a ditch, hurting himself too badly to get up. The servant is wounded, distressed and unable to see clearly. Nothing changes the lord's love for the servant however, and the story ends with the servant being restored to a state of well being and honour.

Julian is adamant that sin does not create wrath in God, separate a person from God, or change the love of God. While she warns against using this as an excuse to do evil, Julian's general approach to the state of sin is refreshing, restoring and non-judgmental in comparison with some other views expressed in the Christian tradition.

Julian also recommends that readers avoid dwelling on other people's sin, as it creates 'a mist on the eye of the soul' that causes a block, an annoyance, a 'tempest' within, that prevents one from seeing God.

Above all, Julian focuses on love and goodness, into which she perceives herself and all her 'even cristen' being 'oned' and knitted, or increased into a state of fulfilment, joy and bliss. The *Showings* demonstrate her as a great teacher, in her ability to document and explain her understanding of a process in which all humankind and creation is being worked into the one fabric of the being that is God, that is love and goodness.

READING JULIAN TODAY

Readers have no other way to come to a work, except with their culture, religion, opinions and experience—that is their own way of seeing the world. It is therefore important when reading Julian, to keep her medieval world and outlook in mind, and to remember that she was speaking out of her particular Christian tradition and culture. Some of Julian's ideas are steeped in medieval Christian teachings, and may seem difficult for modern readers to access. Woven throughout all the revelations however, are ideas and words that bring inspiration and comfort, which transcend the specific framework in which they were expressed.

It is also important when considering different themes and excerpts of Julian's work, not to isolate them from each other. Julian's thought is intricately connected, one idea cannot be held without others. This book has been divided into chapters around themes, but all the themes and ideas are related and work together.

The thoughts and selections in Part Two do not claim to read Julian's mind or pin down exact meanings for her text. The aim is to provide readers with a glimpse of Julian of Norwich and her revelation of love, and to highlight some themes and ideas that she raises which are significant today. These include the concept of God being in all things; the interconnectedness of all things; the belief that what is good and what is love is God; the presence of the divine in creation and humanity; and the understanding that love is the meaning of existence.

NOTE ON TRANSLATIONS

While it is preferable to read a work in its original language and entirety, this small book can only provide excerpts from Julian's text. Every attempt has been made to keep the meaning, feeling and rhythm of her work, including some words no longer commonly used. Two excerpts in each chapter are kept in

Middle English, quoted from *A Book of Showings to the Anchoress Julian of Norwich,* edited by E. Colledge and J Walsh. The modern English excerpts have been translated from this edition.

It must be noted that Julian of Norwich, while having many universal insights, nevertheless reflects the language and outlooks of her era, which at times may jar on modern ears. While using mother imagery for God and especially Christ, Julian still uses the terms 'father, son and holy ghost' and the masculine pronoun for each person of the Trinity, rather than more gender neutral terms. In my discussion and introductions I refer to the 'holy ghost' as 'Holy Spirit', and at times describe the Trinity as Creator, Redeemer, Holy Spirit. I have used upper case for the first letter of certain words (e.g. God, Trinity, Passion, Church) where the Middle English does not. Note also that Julian's words sometimes have more than one meaning, depending on the context. She also uses words not so common today. Readers may find the terms in the Glossary on page 127 useful to hold in mind while reading this book.

The decoration and calligraphy in this book are in the style of manuscript illustration from Julian's time, with modern influences. The decorative feature letters use the same colours as some manuscripts of the *Showings*. The flowers and plants illustrated relate to each chapter, in some cases as traditional emblems, otherwise as thematic symbols.

The hazelnut represents Julian's significant vision of the same. The passionflower represents Christ's Passion, including the crown of thorns (crown), nails (styles), wounds (five stamens) and vinegar soaked sponge (ovary). The hollyhock and dogrose used for 'Christ our Mother' are emblems of beauty, pleasure, pain and fecundity; the iris (communication) and lily (purity, naturalness, sweetness) reflect aspects of 'soul, substance and sensuality'; and the violet symbolises comfort and sympathy. The life and fruit of prayer is illustrated in the harvest scene, overarched by both day and night. Finally, for 'Love is the meaning' the many summer flowers found in the fields of Julian's country represent the coming together and flourishing of numerous meanings and creative expressions found in the *Showings*, including homeliness, simple goodness, love, beauty, bliss and the value of the smallest thing.

PART TWO

The Gift of the Showings

I
it am
That is
All

Julian's God is the ultimate being, 'the endlessness,' the source of everything, enclosing all and in all. 'I it am, I it am, I it am that is all'. Julian describes and experiences God in macro and micro magnifications, as the creator and mid point of all things, no matter how big or small.

God is at once the highest, most awesome being, worthy of worship. At the same time, God is the most 'homely', simple and natural friend. God encompasses all of existence and is everlasting—an expanding universe of Love. At the same time God is present in the tiniest object, point or a second of time.

God is maker, keeper, lover. As maker, 'God has made all that is made.' As keeper, God encloses everything and protects it, keeping it securely in goodness. As lover, God cherishes and loves all that is made.

And who is this God? God is all that is good. In this goodness 'is all the whole, and there truly nothing fails'. Out of this goodness God makes and restores humans, and 'is the very rest' and the 'very peace' for the soul. Whatever is not good, is not of God.

God's being is like a knot, a 'onehead' or oneness to which humans are joined, 'knitted' and 'oned'. Humans, together with the largest and tiniest objects in creation are part of a greater scheme, with all the elements inter-woven into this divine oneness, goodness and love.

Julian also describes God as the 'ground' of all things, which strongly establishes God as the source, strength and sustainer of all. The ground is a foundation for cities, homes, cathedrals. It is the slime or silt that Julian refers to when describing the creation of humans from matter. It is the soil through which rivers run and which people toil over in order to produce food; it is the source of nourishment for trees and other plants. It is the mother of nature, giving life, transforming, receiving. Everything comes from and returns to the ground.

As ground of all, God is the very is-ness, or being-ness of all life and existence, permeating all things. Julian's words 'I it am' echoes the Biblical name of 'I am who I am' as 'the only name of God', declared to Moses (Exodus 3:14) and repeated in various forms throughout the Bible. The words speak of the freedom and essence of God—'I will be who I will be'.

The sense of this ultimate, natural essence is encapsulated in Julian's use of the word 'kind' which can mean: nature, as in the essence or kind of a being (noun); and naturalness or kindness (adjective). God is kind in both ways. By existing in God, humans experience the 'I it am' of God, the 'kind' of God (which is unmade, it exists naturally); and the 'kind' of themselves (which is made of God)—I am who I really am because I am in God. The awareness of this being-ness is a form of prayer, of being in God fully knowing, beholding and seeing.

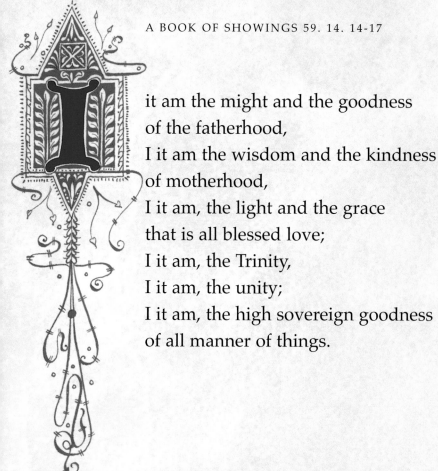

it am the might and the goodness
of the fatherhood,
I it am the wisdom and the kindness
of motherhood,
I it am, the light and the grace
that is all blessed love;
I it am, the Trinity,
I it am, the unity;
I it am, the high sovereign goodness
of all manner of things.

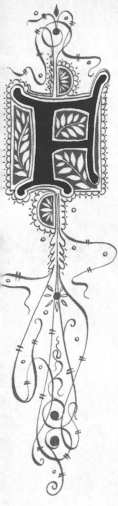

For truly it is the most joy
that may be,
as to my sight,
that he who is highest and mightiest,
noblest and worthiest,
is lowest and meekest,
most homely and most courteous.

I saw god in a poynte, that is to say in my vnderstandyng, by which syght I saw that he is in althyng.

I saw God in a point, that is to say in my understanding, by which sight I saw that he is in all things.

God is alle thyng that is good, as to my syght, and the goodnesse that alle thyng hath, it is he.

God is everything that is good, as to my sight, and the goodness that all things have, it is he.

God is natural in his being;
that is to say
that goodness that is natural,
it is God.
He is the ground,
he is the substance,
he is the same thing
that is nature,
and he is very father
and very mother of nature.

See I am God.
See, I am in all things.
See, I do all things.
See, I never take my hands
from my works,
and never shall without end.

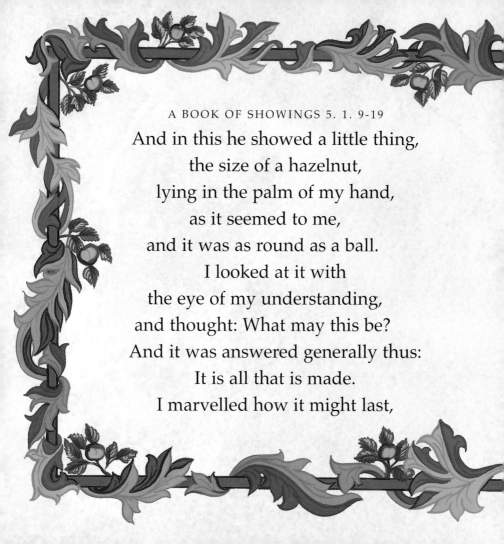

And in this he showed a little thing,
the size of a hazelnut,
lying in the palm of my hand,
as it seemed to me,
and it was as round as a ball.
I looked at it with
the eye of my understanding,
and thought: What may this be?
And it was answered generally thus:
It is all that is made.
I marvelled how it might last,

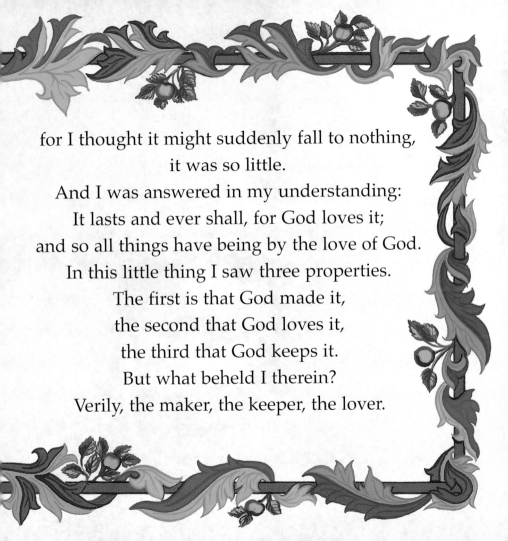

for I thought it might suddenly fall to nothing,
it was so little.
And I was answered in my understanding:
It lasts and ever shall, for God loves it;
and so all things have being by the love of God.
In this little thing I saw three properties.
The first is that God made it,
the second that God loves it,
the third that God keeps it.
But what beheld I therein?
Verily, the maker, the keeper, the lover.

Three
persons
One
Truth

At the heart of Julian's visions is her understanding of God as Trinity, conceived not only as the source of all being ('Father' or Creator), but also as the one who becomes human through Jesus Christ ('Son' or Redeemer), and who in the operation of the Holy Spirit, works continually in the human soul. The framework of 'three persons, one truth' connects various meanings and patterns within the *Showings*, and is the lattice of three through which Julian understands God's relationship with humanity.

The three persons of the Trinity or God—Creator, Redeemer and the Holy Spirit—are in ongoing relationship with the human soul, mind and body. We are constantly 'being worked on' with love, grace, mercy, peace and kindness, so that our 'being' and 'increasing' are brought into 'fulfilment'. God, as the 'Father' is always with us in love and being, the Son 'Jesus Christ' is always 'increasing' our being by the restoring, redeeming power of the Passion, and the Holy Spirit is always drawing the soul into fulfilment. Thus 'our substance is whole in each Person of the Trinity, who is one God.'

In our unity with Christ through the Incarnation and Passion humans and the whole of creation are brought into unity with the Trinity. When Christ 'falls' into the womb of Mary and thus into humanity, Christ's position within the Trinity draws every man and woman back into the Godhead. We are thus 'knit' into the same knot that connects Christ with the Trinity. For

44

Julian the whole working and process of the Trinity connecting with humanity 'is comprehended in Christ'.

Throughout her text, Julian groups her ideas in threes, tying each one back to the 'ground' of the Trinity. Attributes such as grace, love and mercy relate one each to the Creator, Redeemer and the Holy Spirit (Father, Son, Holy Ghost).

We see this in Julian's interpretation of the message 'I may make all things well, and I can make all things well, and I will make all things well, and I shall make all things well … you shall see yourself that all manner of things shall be well'. By 'may' Julian understands the 'Father', by 'can' she understands the 'Son', by 'will' she understands the Holy Spirit, and by 'shall' she understands the unity of the Trinity, and by 'you shall see yourself' she understands the 'oneing' of humanity within the Trinity.

According to Julian, our relationship with the Trinity is ever increasing, through being unified, knitted and 'oned' (being made one) with the divinity. This is the reality each man and woman lives in, but we do not always recognise it. In the Trinity is also the 'oneing of all humankind,' the knitting and unifying of humanity deep within God. Thus the one is also many, and all are interconnected. The infinite diversity of nature and creation is brought into communion through the infinite substance and nature of God as Trinity.

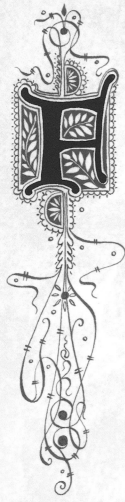

or the Trinity is God,
God is the Trinity.
The Trinity is our maker,
the Trinity is our keeper,
the Trinity is our everlasting lover,
the Trinity is our endless joy
and our bliss,
by our Lord Jesus Christ,
and in our Lord Jesus Christ.

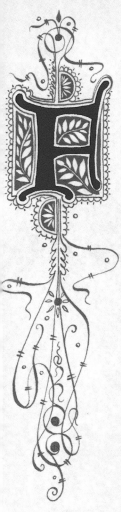

For the almighty truth of the Trinity
is our father,
for he made us
and keeps us in him.
And the deep wisdom of the Trinity
is our mother,
in whom we are enclosed.
And the high goodness of the Trinity
is our lord,
and in him we are enclosed
and he in us.

Alle oure lyfe is in thre: in the furst we haue oure beyng, and in the seconde we haue oure encresyng, and in the thyrde we haue oure fulfyllyng.

...all our life is in three: in the first we have our being, and in the second we have our increasing, and in the third we have our fulfilling.

48

Oure soule is
a made trynyte
lyke to the vnmade
blessyd trynyte,
knowyn and lovyd
fro with out
begynnyng, and in
þe makyng onyd
to the maker . . .

Our soul is a made trinity in the likeness of the unmade blessed Trinity, known and loved since before time began, and in the making oned to the maker.

hus in our Father God almighty
we have our being
and in our mother of mercy
we have our reforming
and our restoring,
in whom our parts be oned
and all made perfect...
and by yielding
and giving in grace of the Holy Ghost
we are fulfilled.

e are enclosed in the Father,
and we are enclosed in the Son,
and we are enclosed in the Holy Ghost.
And the Father
is enclosed in us,
the Son is enclosed in us,
and the Holy Ghost
is enclosed in us,
all might,
all wisdom,
and all goodness,
one God, one Lord.

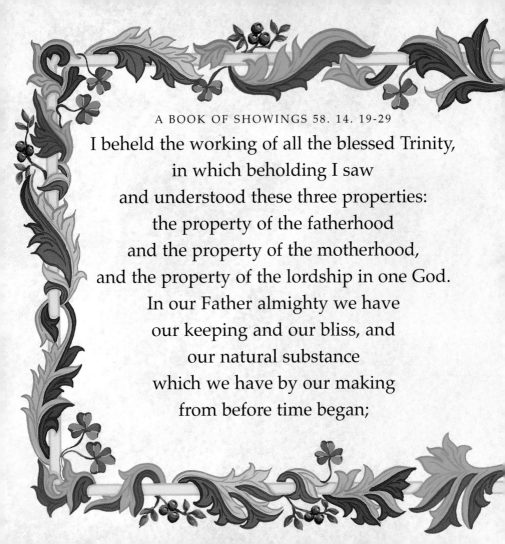

A BOOK OF SHOWINGS 58. 14. 19-29

I beheld the working of all the blessed Trinity,
in which beholding I saw
and understood these three properties:
the property of the fatherhood
and the property of the motherhood,
and the property of the lordship in one God.
In our Father almighty we have
our keeping and our bliss, and
our natural substance
which we have by our making
from before time began;

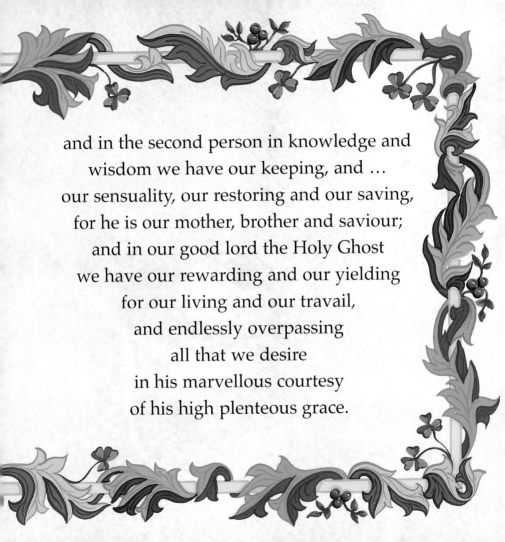

and in the second person in knowledge and
wisdom we have our keeping, and …
our sensuality, our restoring and our saving,
for he is our mother, brother and saviour;
and in our good lord the Holy Ghost
we have our rewarding and our yielding
for our living and our travail,
and endlessly overpassing
all that we desire
in his marvellous courtesy
of his high plenteous grace.

Mind
of
the
Passion

Julian's visions spring from contemplating Christ's Passion. Her descriptions of Christ's dying and tortured body are intensely detailed and realistic. These reflect aspects of medieval experience and spirituality. Suffering and death, often torturous either through violent cruelty or the absence of medical treatment to alleviate pain, were common experiences in daily life.

These realities and especially the impact of the plague on people's psyches are perhaps part of the reason why the deep emotion and drama of the crucifixion became a subject of such intense devotion during the twelfth century and onwards. As a consequence, many individuals desired to experience the Passion through their own physical pain or illness, believing that by imitating Christ's suffering they would come to understand his pain and thereby draw closer to God. Part of this intense devotion included a deep empathy with Christ's mother and friends, in their experience of the Passion story.

This explains why as a young woman Julian prayed for three things—to receive an illness, a 'wound of longing' for God, and the ability to understand Mary's pain at the foot of the Cross. Julian interprets her serious illness at the age of thirty as the answer to this prayer.

All the showings Julian received at this time and her interpretations of them come together in the Passion. She sees the body of Christ as 'the remedy' for woe, sin, and all that is not good. The Passion holds in it all the power and significance of the Incarnation, Resurrection and Ascension. By Christ's body the divine both enters humanity, and brings humanity back into God. The Passion is the ultimate gift of 'again-making' and transformation that returns everything to a natural state of bliss and love in God. The body of Christ in the Passion is the key to humanity and all things being 'oned' with God.

For Julian the Passion also holds in it the extremes of pain and bliss. The devil, so menacing to Julian in some revelations, is by the Passion scorned and brought to nothing, which makes her laugh out loud. An unexpected moment of joy interrupts fear and death. Darkness becomes light. This echoes Julian's understanding that during the Passion all creation was cast into shadow, and suffered. There was an eclipse at physical and spiritual levels—but it passed, and everything was re-consumed in light and love.

Julian develops this paradox in her vision of Christ, now suffering, now in bliss. For her the Passion is an experience of suffering, transformation, and joy. It is a deep manifestation of the Trinity—'for where Jesus is the blessed Trinity is understood'.

For Julian the Passion is not an isolated historical event but an ever present reality. Christ is the 'knot' that draws all the threads together into the greater weave of the Trinity, making the Passion a point of 'great oneing between Christ and us'.

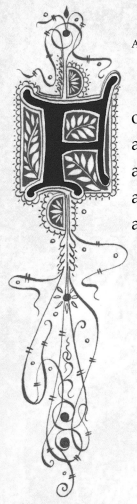

or he is the endless being
and he made us only to himself
and restored us by his precious Passion,
and ever keeps us in his blessed love;
and all this is of his goodness.

here saw I a great oneing
between Christ and us,
to my understanding;
for when he was in pain,
we were in pain,
and all creatures who might suffer pain
suffered with him …
The firmament, the earth,
failed in their nature for sorrow,
in the time of Christ's dying.

In mercy he reformyth vs and restoryth, and by the vertu of his passion, his deth and his vprysing onyd vs to oure substannce . . .

… in mercy he reforms us and restores us, and by the virtue of his Passion, his death and his uprising oned us to our substance …

Alke the souls that shalle be savyd in hevyn with out ende be knytt in this knott and onyd in this oonying, and made holy in this holynesse.

...all the souls that shall be saved in heaven without end be knit in this knot and oned in this oneing and made holy in this holiness.

or in that same time
that God knitted him to our body
in the maiden's womb,
he took our sensual soul,
in which taking,
he having us all enclosed in him,
he oned it to our substance.

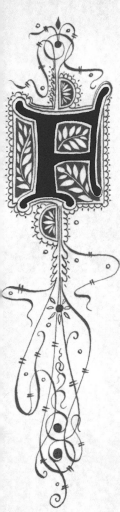

For it is God's will
that we have true delight
with him in our salvation,
and therein he wills that we be
mightily comforted and strengthened,
and thus wills he joyfully
that our soul be occupied with his grace.
For we are his bliss,
for in us he delights without end;
and so shall we in him
with his grace.

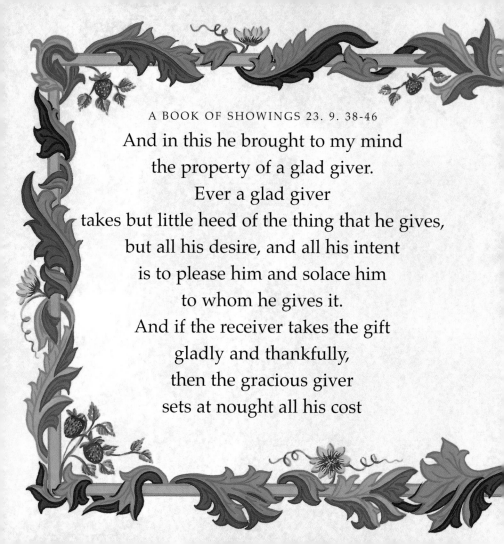

And in this he brought to my mind
the property of a glad giver.
Ever a glad giver
takes but little heed of the thing that he gives,
but all his desire, and all his intent
is to please him and solace him
to whom he gives it.
And if the receiver takes the gift
gladly and thankfully,
then the gracious giver
sets at nought all his cost

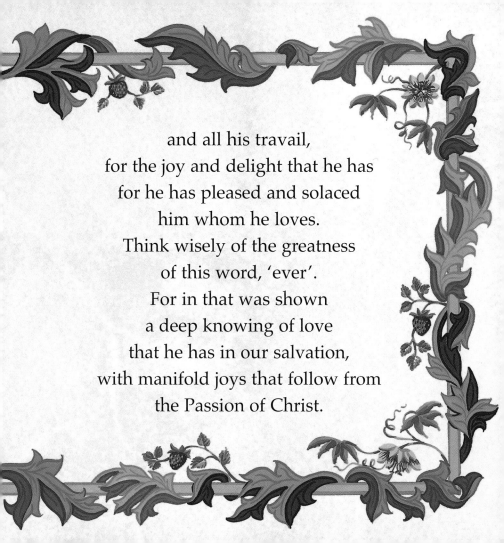

and all his travail,
for the joy and delight that he has
for he has pleased and solaced
him whom he loves.
Think wisely of the greatness
of this word, 'ever'.
For in that was shown
a deep knowing of love
that he has in our salvation,
with manifold joys that follow from
the Passion of Christ.

Christ
is
our
Mother

J ulian highly regards the roles and 'properties' or nature of motherhood, which include 'nature, love, wisdom and knowing, and it is good.' She is well known for representing Christ as 'very mother of life and of all.' Despite this feminine imagery, she writes 'He is our mother', which might seem odd to modern readers! It is not so strange in medieval and earlier texts, where God is sometimes referred to as mother and the masculine pronoun is still used. Images that connect Christ with mothering are not uncommon in medieval writings and artworks. Through Christ's flesh, humans are 're-birthed' or redeemed into completion. Christ is the nourisher and the carer, 'suckling' humans at his bleeding side.

These images echo archetypal mother figures who hold both birth and death—Mother Earth gives life and receives it back at death, Mother Mary is both Madonna, and Pietà. The medieval focus on the Passion brings Christ's body into this tradition. Christ's flesh is a maternal threshold, the divine-human mother body that holds all things in life and death, restoring them into the being of God.

Julian developed these themes in depth. For her, motherhood is a property of each 'person' in the Trinity. God is the ground of motherhood. 'As verily as God is our father, verily is God our mother.' Christ is also our true mother, the ground of our being, through his flesh, nourishment and redemption of humanity. The Holy Spirit is also a mother, working on the

68

human soul to bring it into fulfillment and bliss.

It is Christ, however, who holds all the 'offices of motherhood' in body and attributes. Julian describes the Passion as being like the labour of giving birth. Christ also encloses and keeps the human soul—this too has its mother imagery, of pregnancy, expectancy and protection.

Christ is nourisher and nurturer, who like a mother, leads the child to the breast (his wounded side) and takes on the responsibility, wisdom and care of looking after a child as it grows up. This includes adapting to the child's age and needs, so that it can mature, for example letting the child learn from the challenges of life, and guiding the child without rescuing it inappropriately.

Another important mother role for Christ is that of teacher. Julian regards the *Showings* as her ABC in understanding the mysteries of spirituality. She describes Christ as the mother and teacher of all humanity, including Holy Mother Church.

The image of the human soul as a child is vital to Julian's theology of motherhood, because it brings the divine and the human into dialogue and relationship. She urges her readers to take on the simple properties of childhood. As a child naturally trusts its mother, and 'despairs not of the mother's love', seeking help, comfort, advice and wisdom, so God wills the human soul to come 'seeking, abiding, trusting' in well and woe, with the assurance of a 'homely', wise and loving welcome.

he mother's service is
nearest, readiest and surest:
nearest for it is most of nature,
readiest for it is most of love,
and surest for it is most of truth.

I understood three ways of beholding
motherhood in God.
The first is ground of
making our nature,
the second is taking of our nature,
and there begins
the motherhood of grace,
the third is motherhood in doing.

he wylle then
þat we vse the
properte of a
chylde, that
evyr more kyndly
trustyth to the
loue of þe moder
in wele and in
woo.

...he wills then that we use the property of a child,
that ever more naturally trusts the love of the mother
in well and in woe.

The swet gracious
handes of oure
moder be redy and
diligent a bout
vs; for he in alle
this werkyng
vsyth the very
office of a kynde
norysse . . .

The sweet gracious hands of our mother be ready
and diligent about us; for he in all this working uses
the very role of a kind carer.

The natural loving mother
that understands and
knows the need of her child,
she keeps it full tenderly,
as the nature and condition
of motherhood will.
And ever as it grows
in age and in stature,
she changes her ways of mothering,
but not her love.

The mother may
suffer the child
to fall sometimes,
and be sick in various ways,
for its own benefit,
but she may never suffer
that any manner of peril
come to her child, for love.

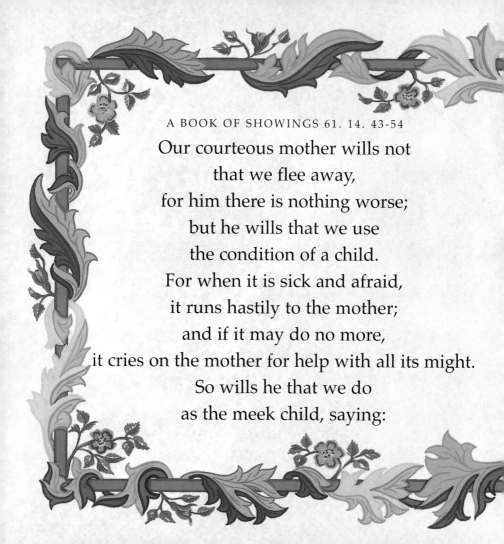

Our courteous mother wills not
that we flee away,
for him there is nothing worse;
but he wills that we use
the condition of a child.
For when it is sick and afraid,
it runs hastily to the mother;
and if it may do no more,
it cries on the mother for help with all its might.
So wills he that we do
as the meek child, saying:

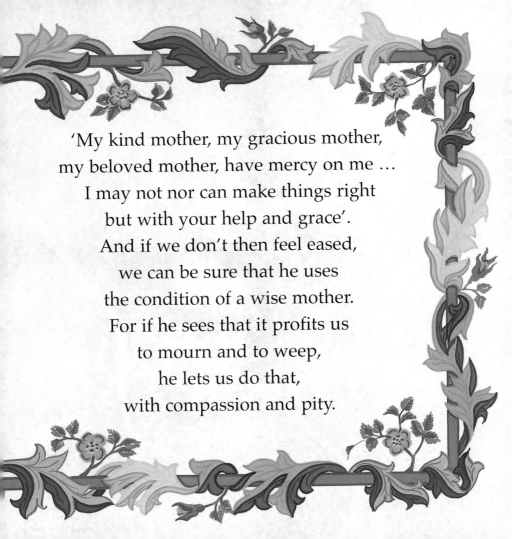

'My kind mother, my gracious mother,
my beloved mother, have mercy on me …
I may not nor can make things right
but with your help and grace'.
And if we don't then feel eased,
we can be sure that he uses
the condition of a wise mother.
For if he sees that it profits us
to mourn and to weep,
he lets us do that,
with compassion and pity.

Soul,
Substance
and
Sensuality

Julian has a complex understanding of the make-up of humans and the Trinity. Hers is an organic spirituality, she does not separate soul and flesh, or what she calls 'substance' and 'sensuality'—all are connected and permeated with each other and God.

The soul 'is made of nothing' but God's own substance, whereas the body is made of 'matter mixed and gathered from all bodily things.' However, while Julian speaks of a 'higher part' of humans that is 'oned' (united) with God, and a 'lower part' that is the flesh, the two are not polar opposites. Both are interconnected through human experience and are 'oned' to God through the flesh of Christ.

'Substance' is the nature of God, the essence of divine being, 'substantial nature unmade'. The human soul's natural substance is 'made of God, and in the same point knit to God'. In this substance 'we are who we are.' Therefore there is nothing between God and the human soul. This means there is 'a substance in us which is never parted from God', and the soul's most natural state is of God.

Julian's term 'sensuality' has a broader meaning than its modern use. It refers to all our sensual nature—our senses and flesh, plus the being and understanding that stems from this. Sensuality is loved and not despised by God. It is enclosed in God who made humans from matter, or 'the silt of the earth.' Sensuality is permeated with God's substance, even though

80

human nature is often 'changeable' and 'muddled', or not in tune with goodness.

Julian does not regard this mixed state or sin as the natural base line of being human. Rather she sees God as the ground, the natural substance in which humans are immersed, despite their frequent contrariness, woe, frailty or sense of isolation. As a plant's roots are in the ground, so is human life in God.

Human brokenness is restored in Christ, the only member of the Trinity who becomes fully sensual. Christ 'again makes' the substance and sensuality of humanity, by knitting it through his own 'sensual soul' (a soul united with flesh) into the Trinity. The aim is not for substance to overcome sensuality, but for both to be fully 'oned' with each other and God.

The substance of humans 'may rightfully be called the soul', and the substance and sensuality *together* is also the soul by its oneing with God. The soul of humans is sensual, as is Christ's soul. Thus the 'Trinity unmade' has elements of substance and sensuality, and this is mirrored in the 'Trinity made', which is the human being. In both God and humans, the substance is in the sensuality and vice versa. 'Our soul is made to be the dwelling place of God,' the 'city' of Christ. 'God is never out of the soul', and the soul is never out of God. This mutual in-dwelling is constant and is so deep, that by knowing and seeing the self clearly, a person comes to know God; and in knowing God, a person comes to know his or her true self.

81

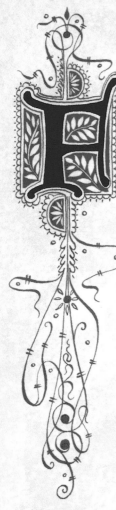

For as the body is clothed in cloth,
and the flesh in skin,
and the bones in flesh,
and the heart in the chest,
so are we, soul and body
clad and enclosed
in the goodness of God.
Yea, and more homely,
for they all vanish and waste away,
the goodness of God is ever whole
and more near to us
without any comparison.

Our soul is oned to him,
unchangeable goodness.
And between God and our soul
is neither wrath nor
forgiveness in his sight.
For our soul is
so fulsomly oned to God
from his own goodness
that between God and our soul
may be right nought.

Oure substannce is in god, and… in oure sensualyte god is, for in the same poynt that oure soule is made sensuall, in the same poynt is the cytte of god.

… our substance is in God, and… in our sensuality God is, for in that same point that our soul is made sensual, in the same point is the city of God.

In whych cytte he
comyth, and nevyr
shall remeve it,
for god is nevyr
out of the soule,
in whych he
shalle dwell
blessydly without
end.

In which city he comes, and never shall leave it, for
God is never out of the soul, in which he shall dwell
blessedly without end.

hether we are stirred to know God
or our soul,
it is both good and true.
God is nearer to us than our own soul,
for he is ground in which our soul stands,
and he is the means that keeps the
substance and the sensuality together,
so that they shall never separate.
For our soul sits in God in very rest,
and our soul stands in God
in sure strength,
and our soul is naturally
embedded in God in endless love.

t is readier to us and more easy
to come to the knowing of God
than to know our own soul.
For our soul is so deep grounded in God
and so endlessly treasured
that we may not come
to the knowing thereof
till we have first knowing of God,
who is the maker to whom it is oned...
I saw that we naturally desire in fullness
wisely and truly to know our own soul,
whereby we are taught to seek it
where it is, and that is into God.

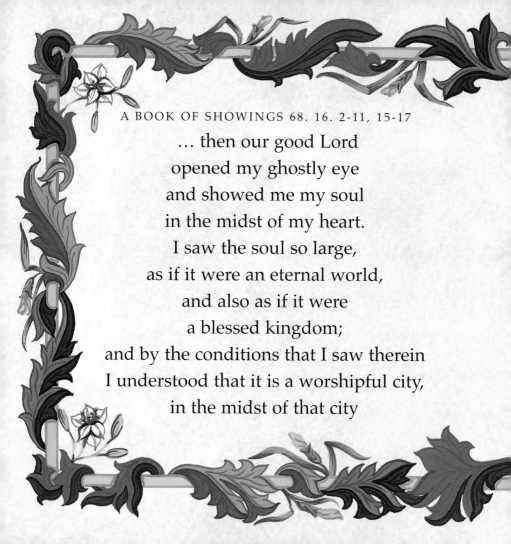

… then our good Lord
opened my ghostly eye
and showed me my soul
in the midst of my heart.
I saw the soul so large,
as if it were an eternal world,
and also as if it were
a blessed kingdom;
and by the conditions that I saw therein
I understood that it is a worshipful city,
in the midst of that city

sits our Lord Jesus,
very God and very man …
He sits in the soul
very calm in peace and rest,
and he rules and judges heaven and earth
and all that is...
The place that Jesus takes in our soul
he shall never leave without end,
as to my sight,
for in us is his homeliest home
and his endless dwelling.

For Julian, prayer is mutual, loving communication between the Trinity and the human soul. Prayer is a dance of the soul with its maker, keeper, lover. It is also an 'understanding of that fullness of joy' to come, a 'true longing and secure trust'. Prayer is a natural yearning of the soul inspired by the Holy Spirit, and God welcomes the soul that comes simply, naturally, 'plainly and homely', without affectation or complex words.

Prayer 'springs' from the ground of God, writes Julian. God stirs the soul to pray, so the soul can trust that prayers are received, and responded to, although the soul is not always aware of how often prayers are already answered. 'I am the ground of your prayer and your beseeching' and of all requests, God tells Julian.

As the soul is made of God, there is a substance in everyone that wills to good, and Julian urges readers to 'teach our soul wisely to cleave to the goodness of God.' The goodness of God is itself a prayer which 'created our soul and keeps it alive, and makes it grow in grace and virtue.' Cleaving to this goodness is a form of prayer in itself, which has much more value than using intermediaries or doing things to get close to God.

For Julian, prayer is a kind of soul breathing. As the soul dwells in God, its very existence is a form of prayer, in well and in woe. This is not always recognised however, and Julian speaks of the need to behold God, to understand that God is, and to enter this state of being-ness simply, reverently, honestly. In this process, prayer becomes 'a witness' that the will of the soul and God are one, and so the conscience is comforted, the soul is 'enabled to grace', and the troubled person is brought into peace.

Julian speaks of 'seeking' and 'beholding' as different experiences of prayer. Beholding is an 'unperceivable' kind of prayer, a communion rather than seeking or beseeching. It requires no words, because the soul is aware of its connection with God. In times of trouble or barrenness of the soul, however, the soul does not always see God, and then prays with words, or calls on God. This seeking 'ones' the soul to God, even if a person feels no sense of God, or no benefit from the prayer. Seeking and beholding are not better than each other, but different ways of being in God. Thus Julian urges people to pray continually, and to 'seek into beholding.'

The end point of prayer is to be 'oned and like to God in all things.' Prayer restores the soul to God, and makes it like God. It is a 'true and gracious, lasting will of the soul,' which is 'oned and fastened' into the will of God.

Julian believes that Christ is the first person of the Trinity to receive prayers, and that Christ brings them into the community of God and the community of souls to be blessed. The joy, thanks and bliss in enjoying a prayer extend beyond the one soul praying, to the Trinity and the whole community of souls.

Prayer ones the soul to God,
for though the soul
be ever like God
in nature and in substance
restored by grace,
it is often unlike
in condition by sin
on man's part.

he wants us to have
true knowing that in himself
he is being;
and in this knowing
he wills that our understanding
be grounded with all our might
and all our intent
and all our meaning.
And in this ground
he wills that we take
our place and dwelling.

God of thy good-
nes geue me thy
selfe, for thou art
inough to me . . .
if I aske anie
thing that is lesse,
ever me wanteth
. . . only in thee
I haue all.

God of your goodness give me your self, for you are
enough for me...if I ask anything that is less, ever I
am wanting...only in you I have all.

The sekyng with feyth, hope and charitie plesyth oure lord, and the fyndyng plesyth the sowle, and fulfyllyth it with joy.

The seeking with faith, hope and charity pleases our Lord, and the finding pleases the soul, and fulfils it with joy.

97

It is more worship to God,
and more true delight
that we faithfully pray to himself
for his goodness,
and cleave thereto by his grace
with true understanding
and steadfast belief,
than if we used all the intermediaries
that heart may think of.
For if we use all these intermediaries
it is too little …
but in his goodness is all the whole,
and there right nothing fails.

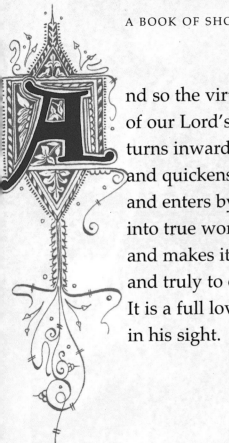

nd so the virtue
of our Lord's word
turns inwards to the soul
and quickens the heart
and enters by his grace
into true working,
and makes it to pray full blessedly,
and truly to enjoy in our Lord.
It is a full lovely thanking
in his sight.

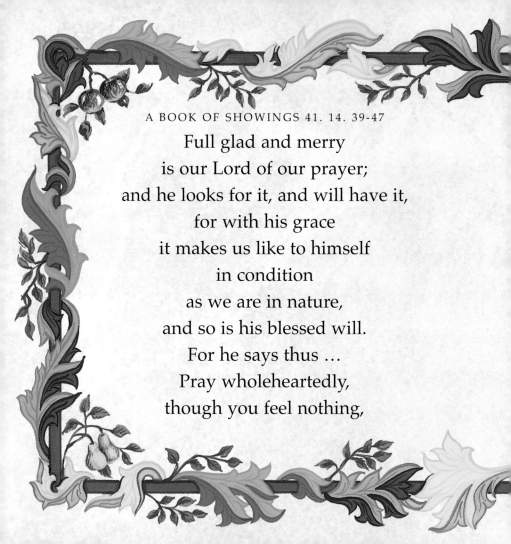

Full glad and merry
is our Lord of our prayer;
and he looks for it, and will have it,
for with his grace
it makes us like to himself
in condition
as we are in nature,
and so is his blessed will.
For he says thus …
Pray wholeheartedly,
though you feel nothing,

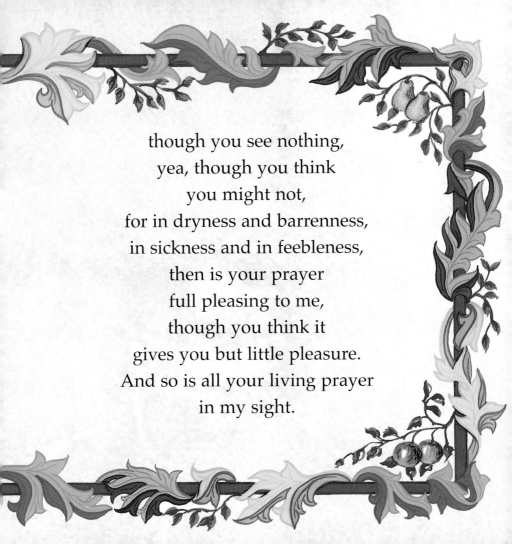

though you see nothing,
yea, though you think
you might not,
for in dryness and barrenness,
in sickness and in feebleness,
then is your prayer
full pleasing to me,
though you think it
gives you but little pleasure.
And so is all your living prayer
in my sight.

Comfort
in Well
and
Woe

Messages of love and comfort permeate the *Showings*—all shall be well, the fiend will be overcome, pain will pass and be brought to nothing, and souls will be united or 'oned' with God in eternal bliss.

Yet Julian is also well aware of struggles in life, of sadness, suffering and a sense of desolation. Central to her work is the understanding that 'for the time of this life we have in us an amazing mixture of well and woe.' The changeable nature of this life gives joy and pain, laughter and fear, disease and health, assurance and doubt.

The love of God however, is unchangeable. No matter what outer or inner turmoil people face, they remain in God, and this is a comfort. Despite her insight, Julian still asks questions, and is puzzled by the promises of bliss. When she receives one of the most famous revelations: 'all shall be well', she asks God 'how shall all be well?'—there is so much hardship and suffering in life, and she has learnt about souls to be damned! God replies 'I will make all things well' because 'what is impossible to you is not impossible to me.'

Julian repeatedly turns to this assurance. She firmly believes that there will be 'a deed' that will make all things well. She holds onto this hope in the face of her pain and that of Christ, the suffering and hardship of people around her, and the upheavals of the Church which she sees 'shaken like a cloth.'

At the heart of this comfort is the pervading love and

goodness of God, which has no blame or wrath and 'treats in us a peace' that lays waste our own wrath. The fiend—which Julian understands to be all that is not love and goodness—is likewise brought to nothing in the presence of goodness. Julian also believes that while sin causes pain, it 'has no substance' (unlike God and goodness) and will be brought to nothing. It is all that is not good and a human experience, rather than a reason for blame or accusation.

Similarly, Julian writes that woe is not always the direct fault of someone, or a consequence of sin. Woe befalls everyone, regardless of what they do. It is part of being human, and sometimes makes life seem like a prison, or penance.

Julian's comfort is the transforming work of love, mercy, grace, peace and goodness which bring her back into peace, and a knowing that she is held in love, and will not perish or be overcome. In highest bliss or deepest sorrow, God is keeping everything 'in like sureness in well and woe.'

This is not a denial of reality but a realisation that human substance is grounded in and 'oned' with God who 'kindles our understanding... directs our ways... eases our conscience... comforts our soul... lightens our heart'. Despite 'wretchedness, debates and strife' humans and all of nature are 'in all ways enclosed' in the goodness and love of God. By this Julian sees that all things are kept surely and transformed, both in a point in time and in the context of eternity.

The remedy is that our Lord
is with us,
keeping and leading us
into fullness of joy.
For this is an endless joy to us …
that he who shall be our bliss
when we are there,
he is our keeper
while we are here,
our way and our heaven
in true love and faithful trust.

hus I saw that God is our very peace,
and he is our sure keeper
when we are ourselves at unpeace,
and he continually works
to bring us into endless peace ...
Suddenly is the soul oned to God,
when she is truly at peace in herself,
for in him is found no wrath.

Thus I sawe
and vnderstood
that oure feyth
is oure lyght
in oure nyght,
whych lyght
is god, oure
endlesse day.

Thus I saw and understood that our faith is our light
in our night, which light is God, our endless day.

108

He wylle that we
be not borne ovyr
lowe for sorows
and tempestys
that falle to vs,
for it hayth evyr
so been before
myracles comyng.

He wills that we be not brought too low with sorrow
and tempests that fall to us, for it has ever been so
before the coming of miracles.

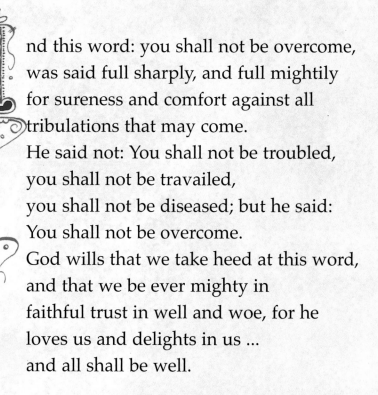

And this word: you shall not be overcome,
was said full sharply, and full mightily
for sureness and comfort against all
tribulations that may come.
He said not: You shall not be troubled,
you shall not be travailed,
you shall not be diseased; but he said:
You shall not be overcome.
God wills that we take heed at this word,
and that we be ever mighty in
faithful trust in well and woe, for he
loves us and delights in us ...
and all shall be well.

t is true that sin
is the cause of all this pain,
but all shall be well,
and all manner of things
shall be well.
These words were shown
full tenderly,
showing no manner of blame to me...

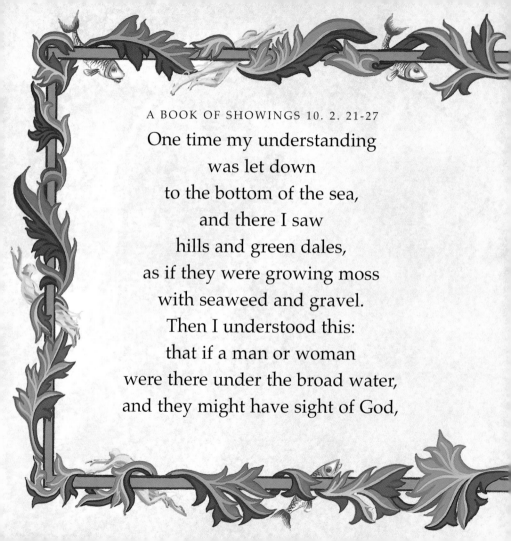

One time my understanding
was let down
to the bottom of the sea,
and there I saw
hills and green dales,
as if they were growing moss
with seaweed and gravel.
Then I understood this:
that if a man or woman
were there under the broad water,
and they might have sight of God,

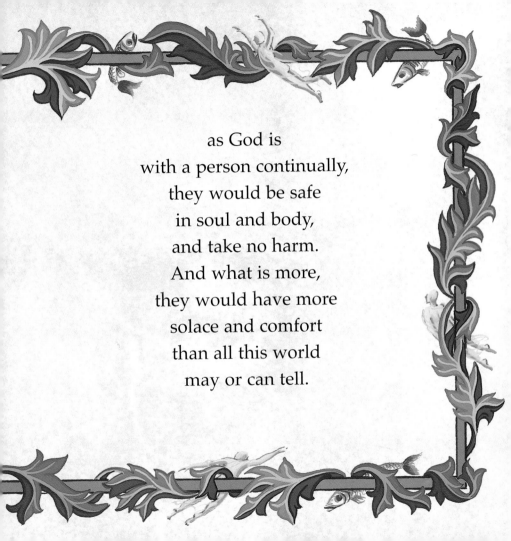

as God is
with a person continually,
they would be safe
in soul and body,
and take no harm.
And what is more,
they would have more
solace and comfort
than all this world
may or can tell.

Love
is
the
Meaning

After her dramatic and deep experience of the *Showings*, Julian asks God the meaning of them. The meaning given to her is simply love. The visions are shown by love, exist by love, are shared for love. Love is the meaning of all existence, and of what Julian understands God to be.

Of all the insight and understanding Julian gains from her visions, the most important is love. God is 'the ground of love'. All persons of the Trinity demonstrate and operate from love. Love is timeless and all encompassing. Love 'was without beginning, is, and shall be without end.' It is the ultimate essence of being. Love is all creative, sustaining, and embracing. Love is the premise of all life, 'all things have their being' by the love of God.

Julian believes that humans are made of God's substance—therefore the true nature of humans is love, not sin, which is a distortion. Out of this true nature comes the soul's desire to seek God, and to love God, 'for before he made us he loved us, and when we were made we loved him.' Humans are called back into this state, or 'restored by love' through Christ.

Love is unchanging, and not lessened or overcome by woe, sin or failings. It is the heart of God's substance, and has no wrath. As there is a constant process of 'oneing' and 'knitting' between the human soul and the Trinity whose three 'persons' enclose and are enclosed within the human, there is no separation between the soul, flesh and love. The human is made for love and endlessly kept in love.

This love is keenly aware, like that of the careful and wise mother, always being concerned for the well being of the child, including its need to learn from life experiences. It is the dance between mother and child. Love is an ever present light, an ongoing heartbeat. An important aspect of this love is 'homeliness'—friendliness, familiarity, and closeness—in which God is 'all that is good and comfortable'. Julian senses that God genuinely delights in humans, 'for he loves us and delights in us, and all shall be well.'

However, this 'homeliness' is not an excuse for careless familiarity or harmful behaviour. In the same way that Julian warns against false angels or destructive people that come in the guise of piety, she tells readers to look at outcomes rather than appearances. Whatever is love, peace and goodness is of God. Whatever undermines these is not of God.

Julian calls everyone to dwell in love, within their own soul, with other people and in the Trinity. In beholding this love she comes to understand and experience her own 'being, increasing and fulfilling', her own 'oneing' with that divine love that has no end and no beginning. This is the love that *is*, the 'I am', the mid point, the ground of all, out of which all things have come and into which everything will go, and in which all things exist. The gift of the *Showings* is the inspiration to behold this love, be in it and continue to generate it.

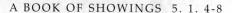

he is our clothing,
that for love wraps around us
and winds around us,
embraces us
and all encloses us,
drapes around us for tender love,
that he may never leave us.
And so in this sight
I saw that he is everything that is good,
as to my understanding.

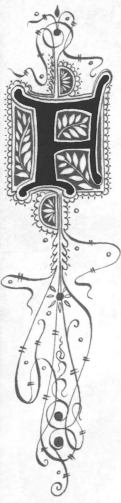

or he is God,
he is good, he is truth,
he is love,
he is peace ... not to be wrathful.
For I saw truly that it is
against the property of his might
to be wrathful ...
God is that goodness
that may not be wrathful,
for God is nothing but goodness.

For this was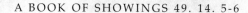
shewed, that oure
lyfe is alle
grounded and
rotyd in loue,
and without
loue we may
nott lyve.

For this was shown, that our life is all grounded and
embedded in love, and without love we may not live.

In this endlesse loue mannis soule is kepte hole ... In whych endlesse loue we be ledde and kepte of god, and nevyr shalle be lost.

... in this endless love our soul is kept whole...in which endless love we be led and kept by God and never shall be lost.

121

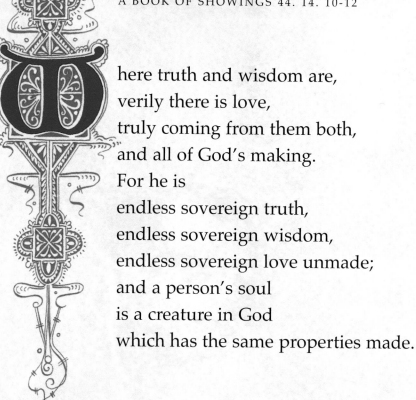

There truth and wisdom are,
verily there is love,
truly coming from them both,
and all of God's making.
For he is
endless sovereign truth,
endless sovereign wisdom,
endless sovereign love unmade;
and a person's soul
is a creature in God
which has the same properties made.

And in this love he has done
all his works,
and in this love
he has made all things profitable to us,
and in this love our life is everlasting.
In our making we had beginning,
but the love wherein he made us
was in him from before time began.
In which love we have our beginning,
and all this shall we see
in God without end.

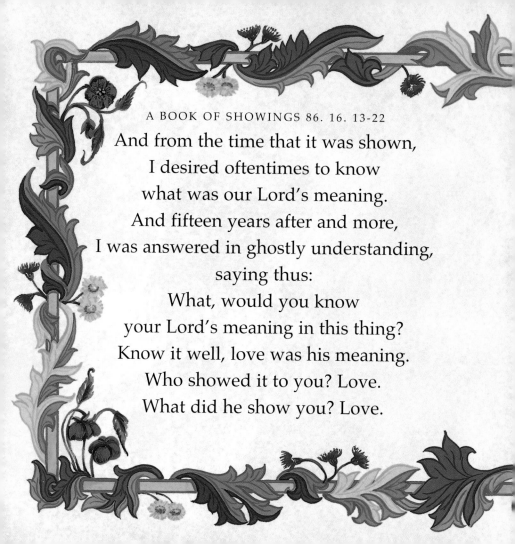

A BOOK OF SHOWINGS 86. 16. 13-22

And from the time that it was shown,
I desired oftentimes to know
what was our Lord's meaning.
And fifteen years after and more,
I was answered in ghostly understanding,
saying thus:
What, would you know
your Lord's meaning in this thing?
Know it well, love was his meaning.
Who showed it to you? Love.
What did he show you? Love.

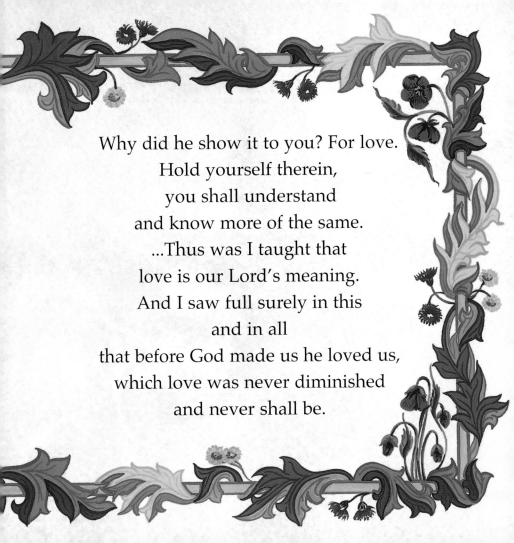

Why did he show it to you? For love.
Hold yourself therein,
you shall understand
and know more of the same.
...Thus was I taught that
love is our Lord's meaning.
And I saw full surely in this
and in all
that before God made us he loved us,
which love was never diminished
and never shall be.

Further Reading

There are many articles and books about Julian of Norwich and medieval mysticism. Space does not allow for a full bibliography. Karen Manton's text for this book is adapted and updated from her 'The Abject and the Divine, a Re-reading of Julian of Norwich'. Melbourne University unpublished MA thesis, 1992.

Julian's Book of Showings

Showings. (Classics of Western Spirituality) Translated and edited by Edmund Colledge and James Walsh. New York: Paulist Press, 1978

Showings of Love. Translated by J.B. Holloway. Collegeville MN: Liturgical Press, 2003

Revelations of Divine Love. (Penguin Classics) Translated by Elizabeth Spearing. Harmondsworth: Penguin, 1998

Books about Julian of Norwich

Abbott, Christopher. *Julian of Norwich:Autobiography and Theology*. Studies in Medieval Mysticism, 2. Woodbridge: Brewer, 1999 (excellent on Julian's theology)

Bradley, R. Julian's Way: *A Practical Commentary on Julian of Norwich*. San Francisco: Harper Collins, 1992

Hide, Kerrie. *Graced Origins to Graced Fulfilment. The Soteriology of Julian of Norwich*. Collegeville MN: Liturgical Press, 2001

Jantzen, Grace. *Julian of Norwich: Mystic and Theologian*. London: SPCK, 1987

Nuth, Joan. *Wisdom's Daughter: The Theology of Julian of Norwich*. New York: Crossroad, 1991 (a study of Julian's theology with an extensive bibliography)

See also the journals, *Speculum* , and *Mystics Quarterly*

Glossary

Beclosed—enclosed, to be enclosed in

Beholding—a deep contemplation, looking on, longing

Even cristen—fellow Christians, fellow women and men

Ghost, ghostly—spirit, spiritual

Homely; homeliness—familiar, friendly, at ease with; familiarity, friendliness

Kind—nature, natural order (noun); natural, kind, compassionate (adjective)

Knitting—knitting together, deep intertwining and connection to make one fabric

Like—to like, delight in

Oned; oneing—to be united, made whole and one with; the uniting, making one with

Point—a point in time, or a point in space

Sensuality—human state of being, nature and flesh, including all the senses, flesh, understanding, our human make up as it is created 'from' the earth and lives through the body

Substance—the natural substance of God

Trinity made—a human being, created by, made of and reflecting God as the Trinity

Trinity unmade—the Trinity: Father, Son, Holy Spirit (Creator, Redeemer, Spirit)

KAREN MANTON studied Julian of Norwich as part of her MA research thesis at the University of Melbourne, in which she explores connections between medieval and modern women writers.

Karen is a writer, editor and project co-ordinator, and has worked in community arts, education and corporate contexts, with a particular interest in multimedia projects that celebrate the diversity of stories, life experiences and cultures within Australia.

Karen won the Dymocks NT Literary Award (Short Story) in 2003 and her work appears in *True North: Contemporary Writing from the Northern Territory*. She has recently been granted the Eleanor Dark Award from Varuna Writers' House, to complete a Fellowship.

LYNNE MUIR is an outstanding illustrator, calligrapher and book designer with a particular interest in Medieval and Celtic design. She designed and illustrated two other titles in this series, *The Gift of St Benedict*, and *The Gift of St Francis*. Lynne received an Honour Award for her illustrations in the children's book *Australian Owls, Frogmouths and Nightjars*.

As well as being an artist, Lynne is a singer. After many years as a folk-singer, she now enjoys classical singing as an enthusiastic member of the Melbourne Chorale.

Both Karen Manton and Lynne Muir have visited Norwich to research this book. They are grateful to the friends of Julian who made them welcome.